CR.

39

D1468080

THE

NASTIEST THINGS

EVER SAID

ABOUT

DEMOCRATS

THE

NASTIEST THINGS

EVER SAID

ABOUT

DEMOCRATS

Collected and Edited by

Martin Higgins

THE LYONS PRESS

Guilford, Connecticut

An imprint of The Globe Pequot Press

To buy books in quantity for corporate use
or incentives, call **(800) 962–0973, ext. 4551,**
or e-mail **premiums@GlobePequot.com.**

The Lyons Press is an imprint of The Globe Pequot Press.

10 9 8 7 6 5 4 3 2 1

Printed in the United States of America

Designed by Carol Sawyer/Rose Design

ISBN 10: 1-59228-957-6

ISBN 13: 978-1-59228-957-8

Library of Congress Cataloging-in-Publication Data is available on file.

This book is dedicated to my father, John M. Higgins,
a 10th Mountain Division Ski Trooper and highly decorated, disabled
WWII veteran who introduced me to comedy and the greatest comedians:
Milton Berle, Ernie Kovacs, Sid Caesar, Steve Allen, Jonathan Winters, and
Red Skelton. My dad's laughter filled our house and, after years of writing
and performing comedy for a living, I have one persistent desire . . . to hear his
big laugh one more time. I miss you Dad. I hope there's a bookstore in heaven.

CONTENTS

INTRODUCTION

This book, along with its evil-twin companion, The *Nastiest Things Ever Said About Republicans*, neatly carves the American political system into two relatively house-trained animals: the Republican/Conservative/Right and the Democrat/Liberal/Left.

Back in the seventies, Senator S. I. Hayawaka, (D-CA) made this helpful distinction between both major parties: "Republicans are people who, if you were drowning fifty feet from shore, would throw you a twenty-five-foot rope and tell you to swim the other twenty-five feet because it would be good for your character. Democrats would throw you a hundred-foot rope and then walk away looking for other good deeds to do."

Like Groucho Marx once said, "All people are born alike—except Republicans and Democrats."

America's political divide has deepened in recent years. The partisan mood is hostile and increasingly polarized. It's become an

Uncivil War. Sound and fury, indeed. It's 24-7 invective, with rants and name-calling fueled by every conceivable media orifice.

With this collection, I hope to further inflame these emotions as well as buttress the cause of prejudice and proud identity. Make this compilation as your go-to source for quotes about Democrats. It will come in handy whenever you're going up against your left-wing adversaries. Give those loudmouth liberals the lip. Choose a zinger. Let the quotes fly, and stand back. Good luck on the political battlefield.

MARTIN HIGGINS
DENVER, COLORADO
JULY 2006

There are only six Democrats in all of Hinsdale Country . . . and you, you son of a bitch, you ate five of them.

—*Colorado judge, sentencing Alfred E. Packer for cannibalizing five members of a prospecting party in 1874*

Lousy Democrats!

—*Homer Simpson,* The Simpsons

WERE HAPPY DAYS EVER HERE?

So long sad times
So long bad times
We are rid of you at last.
Howdy gay times
Cloudy gray times
You are now a thing of the past . . .

—*"Happy Days are Here Again"*

FOR A POLITICAL PARTY that always talks about the future, Democrats strangely prefer to live in the past. What else can explain their abiding affection for that Tin Pan Alley oldie, "Happy Days are Here Again"?

Oddly enough, the song debuted in 1929, prior to the Great Depression when life in America soon became a whole lot less happy. Three years later, FDR used the song at his first inauguration. But it was World War II—and not the New Deal—that got the country economically back on its feet. Nonetheless, "Happy Days" has been recycled ever since as the fight song for Democratic presidential nominees. And lest we forget, years before she became the liberal voice of Hollywood, Barbra Streisand made a recording of the song in 1963.

So let's stroll down U.S. history's memory lane and check up on some of those happy days when pre-Clinton Democrats occupied the White House.

If he became convinced tomorrow that coming out for cannibalism would get him the votes he surely needs, he would begin fattening a missionary in the White House backyard come Wednesday.

—writer H. L. Mencken, on President Franklin D. Roosevelt

An economic illiterate.

—economist John Maynard Keynes,
on President Franklin Delano Roosevelt

A second-class intellect.
*—Supreme Court Justice Oliver Wendell Holmes,
on President Franklin Delano Roosevelt*

Eleanor is a Trojan mare.
*—Alice Roosevelt Longworth, daughter of President Theodore
Roosevelt, on President Franklin D. Roosevelt's wife*

To err is Truman.

> —*popular saying about President Harry S. Truman*

It defies all common sense to send that roughneck ward politician back to the White House.

> —*Senator Robert Taft, on President Harry S. Truman*

Whenever a fellow tells me he is bipartisan I know he is going to
vote against me.

—*President Harry S. Truman*

The White House is the finest jail in the world.

—*President Harry S. Truman*

The fellow has absolutely no principles. Money and gall is all he has.

—*Senator Barry Goldwater, on President John F. Kennedy*

He's younger than my own son.

—*Soviet leader Nikita Khrushchev, on John F. Kennedy before he was elected president*

Sometimes I wish I just had a summer job here.

—*President John F. Kennedy*

The enviably attractive nephew who sings an Irish ballad for the company and then winsomely disappears before the table-clearing and dishwashing begin.

—*Vice President Lyndon B. Johnson, on President John F. Kennedy*

The one thing I do not want to be called is First Lady. It sounds like a saddle horse.

—Jacqueline Kennedy

That was the Kennedy way: you bit off more than you could chew, and then you chewed it.

—author Gerald Gardner

He skipped the grades where you learn the rules of life.

—Vice President Lyndon B. Johnson,
on Attorney General Robert Kennedy

Bobby Kennedy is so concerned about poverty because he didn't have any as a kid.

—*Ronald Reagan, as California governor*

My brother Bob doesn't want to be in government—he promised Dad he'd go straight.

—*President John F. Kennedy*

People say I am ruthless. I am not ruthless. And if I find the man who is calling me ruthless, I shall destroy him.

>   —*Attorney General Robert F. Kennedy*

He tells so many lies that he convinces himself after a while that he's telling the truth. He just doesn't recognize truth or falsehood.

>   —*Robert F. Kennedy, on President Lyndon B. Johnson*

Hey, hey, LBJ, how many kids did you kill today?
—popular chant by Vietnam War protesters

Hyperbole was to Lyndon Johnson what oxygen is to life.
—White House press secretary Bill Moyers

He doesn't like cold intellectuals around him. He wants people who will cry when an old lady falls down in the street.

—Jack Valenti, White House Special Assistant and founder of the Motion Picture Association of America, on President Lyndon B. Johnson

If one morning I walked on top of the water across the Potomac River, the headline that afternoon would read: "President Can't Swim."

—President Lyndon B. Johnson

There are no favorites in my office. I treat them all with the same general inconsideration.

—President Lyndon B. Johnson

I'm a powerful S.O.B.

—President Lyndon B. Johnson

Being president is like being a jackass in a hailstorm. There's nothing to do but stand there and take it.

—President Lyndon B. Johnson

I want loyalty. I want him to kiss my ass in Macy's window at high noon and tell me it smells like roses. I want his pecker in my pocket.
—*President Lyndon B. Johnson, on qualifications for White House staff positions*

If the American people don't love me, then their descendents will.
—*former President Lyndon B. Johnson, in 1972, shortly before his death*

We are not going to send American boys nine or ten thousand miles away from home to do what Asian boys ought to be doing for themselves.

—President Lyndon B. Johnson, in 1964

The major part of the U.S. military task in Vietnam can be completed by the end of 1965.

—Secretary of Defense Robert MacNamara, in 1965

He could take a bite out of you bigger than a T-bone steak and the very next day he would put his arms around you like a long-lost brother.

—Vice President Hubert Humphrey,
on President Lyndon B. Johnson

Hubert Humphrey talks so fast that listening to him is like trying to read *Playboy* magazine with your wife turning over the pages.

—Senator Barry Goldwater, on the vice president

A treacherous, gutless old ward-heeler who should be put in a bottle and sent out with the Japanese current.

—writer Hunter S. Thompson,
on Vice President Hubert Humphrey

Jimmy Carter as president is like Truman Capote marrying Dolly Parton. The job is just too big for him.

—comedian Rich Little

I would not want Carter and his men put in charge of snake-control in Ireland.

—*Senator Eugene McCarthy, on President Jimmy Carter*

Hey, there's a new face in the White House—I'm sure it's there behind those teeth.

—*Comic Bob Hope, on President Jimmy Carter*

Take Howdy Doody, cut the strings, add the top-hatted Mr. Peanut but lose his monocle. Then graft onto his mug Jiminy Cricket's huge toothy smile. You will arrive at something akin to a Jimmy Carter bobble doll.

—*Martin Higgins*

He is your typical smiling, brilliant, backstabbing, bullshitting southern nut-cutter.

> —*Lane Kirkland, AFL-CIO president,*
> *on President Jimmy Carter*

In another show of America's force to the world, when the Soviets invaded Afghanistan, [President] Carter responded by boycotting the Olympics. And thus was a fearsome blow struck at little fourteen-year-old American girls who had spent their lives training for the Olympics.

> —*author Ann Coulter*

Jimmy's still mad because I wouldn't take the secretary of state. I want to be director of alcohol and firearms.

—*Billy Carter, the president's brother*

His administration has managed the extraordinary feat of having, at one and the same time, the worst relations with our allies, the worst relations with our adversaries, and the most serious upheavals in the developing world since the end of the Second World War.

—*Henry Kissinger, on President Jimmy Carter*

I have looked on a lot of women with lust. I've committed adultery in my heart many times.

—*President Jimmy Carter, in a* Playboy *interview*

Carter was the first politician in memory to come complete with halo.

—*Representative Morris Udall*

Teddy Roosevelt once said, "Speak softly and carry a big stick." Jimmy Carter wants to speak loudly and carry a fly swatter.

—*President Gerald R. Ford*

II

THE CO-DEPENDENT SCHEMERS:
BILL AND HILLARY CLINTON

AS THE FORTY-SECOND PRESIDENT, Bill Clinton excelled as the consummate shuck-and-jive showman. He'd tell any crowd whatever it wanted to hear. In reality, he was a draft-dodging, lying, sexual predator in blackface, kneeling with his Bubba banjo, singing Al Jolson's "Mammy" to America.

Wife Hillary played Bonnie to Bill's Clyde. They honed their unseemly ways in Arkansas's backwaters before hitting the road for bigger political scores. Publicly, they worked well as a team. Privately, they inhabited each other's hell.

Long before Monica waved her thong-bottom at Bill in the Oval Office, the ruthless Hillary made a secret pact with her husband's devil of a libido. She tolerated his wandering eye because her eye was always fixed on the main prize: doing whatever it takes to become the nation's first female president.

For the sake of America, let's certainly hope that doesn't happen.

Stop Mad Cow—No Hillary in 2008

—bumper sticker

The Clintons are the Costco of Sleaze.

—comic Dennis Miller

Bill Clinton is a man who thinks international affairs means dating a girl from out of town.

—author Tom Clancy

We in the Republican Party have never said to the press that
Clinton's a philandering, pot-smoking draft-dodger.
>   —*political strategist and pundit Mary Matalin*

She sounds like a screeching ex-wife.
>   —*radio talk-show host Rush Limbaugh,*
>   *on Senator Hillary Rodham Clinton*

All public figures use makeup to cover a blemish or two. Only Hillary wears a mask of so many layers, one that hides her true face altogether.

> —*Dick Morris, author, pundit, and former Clinton campaign strategist*

When they swore her in, she used the Clinton family Bible. You know, the one with only seven commandments.

> —*David Letterman, host of* Late Night with David Letterman, *on Hillary Clinton becoming New York's junior senator*

Bill Clinton is an unusually good liar.

—Senator Bob Kerrey, in 1996

The road to tyranny, we must never forget, begins with the destruction of the truth.

—President Bill Clinton, in a 1995 speech

Hillary's presidential campaign has a $20 million war chest, but Bill is still more interested in $15,000 silicone chests.

—Martin Higgins

If I were a single man, I might ask that mummy out. That's a good-looking mummy.

> —*President Bill Clinton, looking at an Incan mummy*
> *at the National Geographic museum*

I'm not going to have some reporters pawing through our papers. We are the president.

> —*Former first lady Hillary Clinton,*
> *commenting on the release of*
> *subpoenaed documents during Filegate*

I'm not some little woman standing by my man like Tammy Wynette.
—Hillary Clinton, on being questioned about her husband's infidelity on 60 Minutes, *in 1992*

I think the ethical standards established in this White House have been the highest in the history of the White House.
—Vice President Al Gore, in 1996

Top Democrats have mixed feelings about Senator Hillary Clinton running for president. Apparently, some Democrats don't like the idea, while others hate it.

—Conan O'Brien, host of Late Night with Conan O'Brien

You'd better call my dad. My mom's pretty busy.

—Chelsea Clinton, twelve years old, talking with a nurse at Sidwell School

The president has kept all of the promises he intended to keep.
—Clinton staff aide George Stephanopoulos,
speaking on Larry King Live

Drag a hundred-dollar bill through a trailer park, you never know what you'll find.
—James Carville, after Paula Jones made sexual-harassment
allegations against Bill Clinton

I just got sick and tired of lying for the fella.

*—Jim McDougal, Clinton's business partner
in the Whitewater Scandal*

Senator Hillary Clinton is attacking President Bush for breaking his campaign promise to cut carbon-dioxide emissions, saying a promise made, a promise broken. And then out of habit, she demanded that Bush spend the night on the couch.

—Craig Kilborn, host of The Late Late Show

Ronald Reagan has a story for every occasion. Bill Clinton has
an excuse.

—*pundit Fred Barnes*

It depends on what the meaning of the word "is" is.
   —*President Bill Clinton's grand-jury testimony, responding to a
      question about his affair with Monica Lewinsky*

You may think you have a stressful job, but since she's been a Senator, Hillary Clinton, they say, put on thirty pounds. In fact, she has gotten so heavy that today Bill hit on her.

—*David Letterman*

Hell, if you work for Bill Clinton, you go up and down more times than a whore's nightgown.

—*James Carville*

Clinton's the sort of guy who'll always volunteer to help you move, then when you've got four of ya picking up the sofa, he's the one who'll be fake lifting.

—*Dennis Miller*

Hillary Clinton has a sharp, political mind, until she speaks it.

—*Martin Higgins*

You know why I think she's running? I think she finally wants to see what it's like to sleep in the president's bed.

—Jay Leno on Senator Clinton's 2008 White House bid

Hillary Clinton is repositioning herself constantly. She is now campaigning against sex and violence in TV shows and video games. She said studies show that children who are exposed to sexual images are more likely to blow her husband.

—Bill Maher, host of Real Time with Bill Maher

I have to confess that it's crossed my mind that you could not be a Republican and a Christian.

—*Former first lady Hillary Clinton, interview in the* Richmond Times-Dispatch, *in 1997*

Hillary and Bill Clinton both suffer from a variety of attention-deficit disorders. When they don't get enough attention, they become disordered.

—*Dick Morris*

Vanity Fair reports that former President Clinton and Al Gore haven't spoken to each other since George W. Bush's inauguration. Not only that, Bill and his wife, Hillary, haven't spoken since Richard Nixon's inauguration.

—*Conan O'Brien*

President Bush and Bill Clinton both agree that cloning is morally wrong. Clinton said that he thinks humans should be made the old-fashioned way—liquored up in a cheap hotel room.

—*Jay Leno*

A few more fat old men wouldn't hurt the place.
—*President Reagan's press secretary Marlin Fitzwater,*
on President Clinton's early Cabinet appointees

At the National Portrait Gallery in Washington, D.C., new portraits were unveiled of former President Clinton and first lady Hillary Clinton. The Smithsonian said that the portraits of Bill and Hillary will not hang in the same room. Boy, talk about art reflecting life.
—*Jay Leno*

Everything Hillary has accomplished has come in the wake of her husband's achievements.

—*Dick Morris*

Hillary Clinton was booed in a speech over her Iraq stance. She said she doesn't support an open-ended commitment and she doesn't support setting a date to leave. However, what works in her marriage may not make good foreign policy.

—*comic Argus Hamilton*

They're not my type. I like to be around low-class people like reporters.

> —*former NBA player, Charles Barkley, on why he didn't attend the Clinton inauguration*

The Secret Service has signs all over the island saying, "Please do not feed the president."

> —*David Letterman, on Clinton's vacations on Martha's Vineyard*

Politics gives guys so much power that they tend to behave badly around women. And I hope I never get into that.

> —*Bill Clinton, to a female friend while he was a Rhodes scholar at Oxford*

In an unlikely pairing, Hillary Clinton made an appearance this week with Newt Gingrich to push a health-care plan. The press is making a big deal out of this thing with Newt. But, hey, if anyone knows how to appear in public with a man she can't stand, it's Hillary.

> —*Jay Leno*

Hillary Clinton's victory in the New York Senate race was greeted with disdain by Senate majority leader Trent Lott, who warned that when she gets to the Senate, she'll just be "one of one hundred." To which Hillary responded, "I'm used to being one of one hundred, I'm married to Bill Clinton."

—*Tina Fey*, Saturday Night Live's *"Weekend Update"*

Q. What do O.J. Simpson and Bill Clinton have in common?
A. Both are lying, bad golfers, who leave a trail of DNA behind.

—*Anonymous*

I loved Bill Clinton because he made me a very rich man. When he said he never lied to us, I built a swimming pool in the back of my house. When he said he had an affair with Monica Lewinsky, I bought a new Lexus. When he pardoned Marc Rich, I bought a house on Martha's Vineyard. I was disappointed when the publisher didn't offer me ten million dollars to write my version of these events.

—*humorist Art Buchwald*

Let's face it. If the Clintons' marriage were any more about convenience, they'd have to install a Slurpee machine and a Slim Jim rack.

—*Dennis Miller*

A parasite on the Democratic Party.

> —*writer Camille Paglia, on Senator Hillary Clinton*

Look, half the time when I see the evening news, I wouldn't be for me, either.

> —*President Bill Clinton, in 1995*

Right-wingers said Clinton was a lying, unscrupulous traveling salesman. It turned out he was a lying, unscrupulous traveling salesman. Now liberals scratch their heads demanding to know: So what was it about him you didn't like?

> —*Ann Coulter*

I equate it to an afternoon thunderstorm. There's a lot of thunder and lightning and then it's gone and the sun is shining again.

—*James Carville, on President Bill Clinton's angry tirades*

More problems for [Senator] Hillary Clinton. The head of New York State's leading gay rights group describes Hillary Clinton as a disappointment on same-sex marriage. Today, her husband Bill described her as a disappointment on opposite-sex marriage.

—*Jay Leno*

You got it backwards. You messed around with a Jewish girl, and now you're paying a goyish lawyer. You should have messed around with a goyish girl and gotten a Jewish lawyer.

—White House aide Rahm Emanuel, speaking to
President Clinton after the Monica Lewinsky scandal

Q. What was Lewinsky's code name in the FBI?
A. Deep Throat.

—Anonymous

In an interview on Japanese television, Bill Clinton said Hillary would make a great president—lousy intern but great, great president.

—Jay Leno

III

PIN THE LIBERAL TAIL ON THE DONKEY

HOPELESSLY MIRED IN THE SIXTIES, the Left loves adhering to the illusion of always being right. Just name an issue—god, gays, guns, military—and liberals will trumpet their own moral and intellectual superiority. But underneath their know-it-all preening and smug, intolerant posturing is a stubborn jackass that lacks common sense. It constantly chafes at the bit of reason, and is always attempting to bury its head in the government feedbag.

To best explain this willful obstinacy, one needs look no further than the Democratic Party's unofficial symbol—the donkey. It first came into political use during Andrew Jackson's presidential campaign in 1828. Jackson's campaign slogan was "Let the people rule." Almost 180 years later, the Democrats are still braying and foolishly kicking up a cloud of dust.

The liberals have many tails, and chase them all.

—*H. L. Mencken*

Democrats never agree on anything, that's why they're Democrats.
If they agreed with each other, they would be Republicans.

—*humorist Will Rogers*

Democrats couldn't care less if people in Indiana hate them. But
if Europeans curl their lips, liberals can't look at themselves in
the mirror.

—*Ann Coulter*

The Democrats have the management skills of celery. They're the kind of people who'd stop to help you change a flat, but would somehow manage to set your car on fire.

—humorist Dave Barry

Republicans believe every day is the Fourth of July, but Democrats believe every day is April 15.

—President Ronald Reagan

Al Gore claiming that Earth is "running a fever" as evidenced by global warming, is like taking your overheated car to a mechanic and having him say, "It seems angry about something."

—Martin Higgins

Liberals can understand everything but people who don't understand them.

—comic Lenny Bruce

The Democrats are the party that says government will make you smarter, taller, richer, and remove the crabgrass on your lawn.

—humorist P. J. O'Rourke

Look, I realize this is America—everybody has the right to organize. The Democratic Party should try it sometime.

—*Dennis Miller*

You can never underestimate the ability of the Democrats to wet their finger and hold it to the wind.

—*President Ronald Reagan*

If you liberals keep gettin' your way, we're all gonna hear one big
loud flush. The sound of the U.S. of A. goin' straight down the toilet.
—*Archie Bunker (played by Carroll O'Connor),*
in All in the Family

The sixties were an oyster decade: slippery, luxurious, and reportedly
aphrodisiac, they slipped down the historical throat without touch-
ing the sides.

—*writer Julian Barnes*

Enraging liberals is simply one of the more enjoyable side effects of my wisdom.

—*Rush Limbaugh*

Call me old-fashioned, but a grief-stricken war mother shouldn't have her own full-time PR flack.

—*Ann Coulter, on antiwar activist Cindy Sheehan*

Liberals are generous with other people's money, except when it comes to questions of national survival when they prefer to be generous with other people's freedom and security.

—National Review founder William F. Buckley Jr.

Hollywood is determined to convince America that gay sex is the equivalent of hetero sex, so they portray both as impersonal, violent, degrading, and regrettable endeavors.

—Martin Higgins

I never use the words Democrats and Republicans. It's Liberals and Americans.

—James Watt, former Secretary of the Interior under President Reagan

The Democratic Party is like a horse driving backwards in a railroad car—it never sees anything until it has gone past it.

—Representative Thomas Reed, 1887–1899

This is the first time I have received an invitation to the Democratic headquarters.

—Representative Thomas Reed, after being told by a heckler to go to hell

The Democratic Party is like a mule without pride of ancestry or hope of posterity.

—Representative Emory Speer, 1883

A liberal intellectual is someone who mistakes a beard for a strong jawline.

—*Martin Higgins*

The hippies wanted peace and love. We wanted Ferraris, blondes, and switchblades.

—*musician Alice Cooper, on the sixties*

During my service in the United States Congress, I took the initiative in creating the Internet.

—Vice President Al Gore, speaking to Wolf Blitzer on CNN

Liberals don't so much think as they just blindly believe.

—writer J. J. Lane

In Berkeley, city officials want to rename manhole covers and call them "personhole" covers to foster gender equality. How about a-hole instead?

—Martin Higgins

As for those deserters, malcontents, radicals, incendiaries, the civil and uncivil disobedients among the young, SDS, PLP, Weathermen I and Weathermen II, the revolutionary action movement, the Black United Front, Yippies, Hippies, Yahoos, Black Panthers, Lions and Tigers alike—I would swap the whole damn zoo for a single platoon of the kind of young Americans I saw in Vietnam.

—Vice President Spiro Agnew

Conservatives saw the savagery of 9/11 in the attacks and prepared for war; liberals saw the savagery of the 9/11 attacks and wanted to prepare indictments and offer therapy and understanding for our attackers.

—White House political adviser Karl Rove

Liberals are very broad-minded: they are always willing to give careful consideration to both sides of the same side.

—writer J. J. Lane

I didn't leave the Democratic Party. It left me.

—President Ronald Reagan

Ninety percent of Berkeley voters are Democrats. When the other ten percent is asked what party they support, they look both ways and say, "Uh, why, Democrats, of course!"

—Martin Higgins

A liberal is someone who feels a great debt to his fellow man; which debt he proposes to pay off with your money.

—radio talk-show host G. Gordon Liddy

The Oscars is the one night of the year when you can see all your favorite stars without having to donate any money to the Democratic Party. And it's exciting for the stars as well because it's the first time many of you have ever voted for a winner.

—Jon Stewart, hosting the Academy Awards

A liberal is someone who won't take his own side of an argument.

—*poet Robert Frost*

A liberal is a man who wants to use his own ideas on things in preference to generations who he knows know more than he does.

—*Will Rogers*

Cindy Sheehan is an enigma. She couldn't prevent her son from joining the military, but maybe she can stop yours.

—*Martin Higgins*

Listening to Democrats complain about inflation is like listening to germs complain about disease.

—Vice President Spiro Agnew

Anti-gun advocates who say "Man alone kills for sport" have never owned a cat.

—Martin Higgins

Democrats can't get elected unless things get worse—and things won't get worse unless they get elected.

—*Jeane J. Kirkpatrick, former U.S. ambassador to the United Nations*

There are no liberals behind steering wheels.

—*columnist Russell Baker*

I never said all Democrats were saloonkeepers. What I said was that all saloonkeepers are Democrats.

—nineteenth-century newspaperman Horace Greeley

The Democratic Party is now the party of anger.

—pollster Frank Luntz

I think one of the problems the Democrats have today is that they are an elitist party.

—*Ed Gillespie, former Republican National Committee chairman*

Is he hot? Yeah. Not unless you can give a better [mimicking eating a banana] than me.

—Court TV's *Kimberly Guilfoyle, at a gay-rights fund-raiser, on her now ex-husband, San Francisco mayor Gavin Newsom*

I admire Ted Kennedy. How many fifty-nine-year-olds do you know who still go to Florida for spring break?

—*pundit Patrick Buchanan*

One difference between a liberal and a pickpocket is that if you demand your money back from a pickpocket, he won't question your motives.

—*from* National Review

Liberals are variously described as limousine, double-domed, screaming, knee-jerk, professional, and "bleeding heart."

—*columnist William L. Safire*

Back in the thirties we were told we must collectivize the nation because the people were so poor. Now we are told we must collectivize the nation because the people are so rich.

—*William F. Buckley Jr.*

The Clinton administration launched an attack on people in Texas because those people were religious nuts with guns. Hell, this country was founded by religious nuts with guns. Who does Bill Clinton think stepped ashore on Plymouth Rock?

—P. J. O'Rourke

It's a cliché of punditry that Republicans are the Daddy Party and the Democrats are the Mommy Party. The metaphors are out-of-date. We must look at the Republicans as the Adult Party and the Democrats as naughty children sent to sup at the children's table.

—columnist Suzanne Fields

Congratulations gay people—you are about to discover the joys of alimony.

> —*Craig Ferguson, host of CBS's* Late Late Show, *on a California judge's ruling legalizing gay marriage*

Liberals don't care what you do as long as it's compulsory.

> —*M. Stanton Evans, director of the National Journalism Center*

The Democrats seem stuck in concrete.
> —*Ken Mehlman, Republican National Committee chairman*

A liberal is a man who leaves a room when the fight begins.
> —*writer Heywood C. Broun*

Whenever Senator Ted Kennedy buys a pair of pants, he asks for a belt—usually on the rocks.
> —*Martin Higgins*

The Democrats of the sixties were all about making love and not war while a war-loving Republican is a man who would fight, bleed, sacrifice, and die for his country. Could you imagine what that very same man would do for his wife in the bedroom?

—*Michele Zipp, former editor of* Playgirl

Some say that hardly anyone finds Al Franken funny. I disagree. Visit any asylum and there's always someone laughing at the radio.

—*Martin Higgins*

The sad thing about the sixties was the weak-mindedness of the
so-called radicals and the way that they managed to get co-opted.
I think one of the things that helped that happen was LSD. It's
the only chemical known to mankind that will covert a hippie to
a yuppie.

—musician Frank Zappa

The sixties, of course, was the worst time in the world to try
and bring up a child. They were exposed to all these crazy things
going on.

—former First Lady Nancy Reagan

The other day they asked me about mandatory drug testing. I said
I believed in drug testing a long time ago. All through the sixties, I
tested everything.

—*Boston Red Sox pitcher Bill Lee*

Policemen should shoot arsonists and looters; arsonists to kill and
looters to maim and detain. You wouldn't want to shoot children, but
with mace you could detain youngsters.

—*Mayor Richard J. Daley, giving instructions to*
Chicago police during riots following the assassination
of Martin Luther King Jr. in 1968

I would like to electrocute everyone who uses the word "fair" in connection with income tax policies.

—*William F. Buckley Jr.*

When the Democratic Party forms a firing squad we form a circle.

—*Representative Morris Udall*

Liberal appeasement and pacifism towards terrorists: it's like buying drinks for a belligerent drunk to avoid a fight.

—*Martin Higgins*

A Democratic president is doomed to proceed to his goals like a squid squirting darkness all about him.

—writer Clare Boothe Luce

They are the troubadours and the crooners of catastrophe.

—Clare Boothe Luce, on Democrats

The liberal Democratic men, who have done nothing but blame America and refuse to fight, are rather disgraceful. They're unconscionable wussies, and Republican women know enough to stay clear of this worthless bunch. Give me a Republican man anytime who is for the cause and understands what's at stake.

—*Michele Zipp*

God is a Republican, and Santa Claus is a Democrat.

—*H. L. Mencken*

I went to a free speech and anti-war rally. When I tried to have a discussion with a protester, he told me to shut the f—k up.

—*Martin Higgins*

Some of you may remember that in my early days, I was sort of a bleeding-heart liberal. Then I became a man and put away childish ways.

—President Ronald Reagan

Hippies, hippies. They want to save the world but all they do is smoke pot and play Frisbee.

—Eric Cartman, character on South Park

Children, for whom suburban life was supposed to make wholesome Little Johns and Wendys, became the acid-dropping, classroom-burning hippies of the 1960s.

—*historian Ronald Steel*

Neoconservatives are people who were once liberals but sobered up.

—*R. Emmett Tyrrell Jr., founder of* American Spectator *magazine*

Washington's answer to Barbra Streisand.
—Slate editor Jacob Weisberg, on House minority leader Nancy Pelosi

The Democrats just don't have a foreign policy that they're willing to defend.
—Chris Matthews, host of MSNBC's Hardball with Chris Matthews

It's like being against typhoons.

—*author Tom Wolfe, on the
nuclear freeze movement*

The hippies had in mind something that they wanted, and
were calling it "freedom," but in the final analysis "freedom" is
a purely negative goal. It just says something is bad. Hippies
weren't really offering any alternatives other than colorful short-
term ones, and some of these were looking more and more like
pure degeneracy. Degeneracy can be fun but it's hard to keep up
as a serious lifetime occupation.

—*Robert Pirsig, author of* Zen and the
Art of Motorcycle Maintenance

The Democrats have had no message, no leadership, and they keep blowing every opportunity we give them. And I've told my Democratic friends, if nothing else, just keep your mouths shut and just let us self-destruct. But they won't even let us do that.

—Senator Chuck Hagel

They say Democrats don't stand for anything. That's patently untrue. We do stand for anything.

—Senator Barack Obama, at the 2006 Gridiron dinner

Whenever liberals start droning on about "complex issues" for which there are no "simple solutions," hide Grandma and the kids.

—Ann Coulter

Funny how history repeats itself. John Wilkes Booth was America's favorite actor and George Clooney just won an Oscar.

—Martin Higgins

Bart: But Grandpa, didn't you wonder why you were getting
            checks for doing absolutely nothing?
Grandpa: I figured it was 'cause the Democrats were in power again.

—The Simpsons

Yes, I'm going to be the president of the United States. You know
why? You think you can get chicks by being in the movies? You can
really get chicks by being the president.

—*actor Ben Affleck*

Smoking kills. If you're killed, you've lost a very important part of your life.

—actress Brooke Shields, in an interview to become spokesperson for a federal antismoking campaign

Mick Jagger and I just really liked each other a lot. We talked all night. We had the same views on nuclear disarmament.

—Jerry Hall, aka Mrs. Mick Jagger

You know he's thinking, "I should have made *Super Size Me*—
I've done the research."

—Chris Rock, on filmmaker Michael Moore

It was so sweet backstage, you should have seen it: The Teamsters
were helping Michael Moore into the trunk of his limo.

—Steve Martin, host of the Academy awards

Liberals claim to want to give a hearing to other views, but then are shocked and offended to discover that there are other views.

—*William F. Buckley Jr.*

Yes! I am a citizen! Now which way to the welfare office?

—*Apu,* The Simpsons

Whenever a liberal begins a statement with "I don't know which is more frightening," you know the answer is going to be pretty clear.

—*Ann Coulter*

When liberals say that we live in a police state, it is proof positive that we're not.

—*Martin Higgins*

We're about to enter the sixties again.

—*Democratic National Committee chairman Howard Dean, speaking at a religious conference in 2006*

I do not believe in people owning guns. Guns should be owned only by [the] police and military. I am going to do everything I can to disarm this state.

—*Massachusetts governor Michael Dukakis,
and 1988 Democratic presidential candidate*

Ted Kennedy I don't trust, like I don't trust Nixon, although I think Nixon's done a helluva lot better than I thought he would.

—*Teresa Heinz Kerry, wife of 2004 Democratic
presidential nominee, Senator John Kerry*

A vegetarian is a person who won't eat anything that can have children.

—comic David Brenner

The ratio of left-wing professors in Berkeley and Stanford is seven to one and nine to one. You can't get hired if you're a conservative in American universities.

—author David Horowitz

The Berkeley City Council is the first in the country that voted for Bush's impeachment. But it still can't figure out how to fix its chronic problem with homelessness and street crime.

—Martin Higgins

I knew I'd been living in Berkeley too long when I saw a sign that said "Free Firewood" and my first thought was "Who was Firewood and what did he do?"

—*writer and painter John Berger*

I am here to interview Fidel for Spanish television.

—*filmmaker Oliver Stone, in Havana*

If you can remember anything about the sixties, you weren't really there.

—*musician Paul Kantner*

The freedom that women were supposed to have found in the Sixties largely boiled down to easy contraception and abortion; things to make life easier for men.

—*British columnist Julie Burchill*

A party of doom and gloom.

—Vice President Dan Quayle,
on the Democrats

Hell hath no fury like a liberal scorned.

—comic Dick Gregory

My father always said: If it is on the table, eat it.

—Senator Edward Kennedy

People today are still living off the table scraps of the sixties.

—musician Bob Dylan

Annoy a Liberal—Work hard and be happy.

—bumper sticker

I do unto others what they do unto me, only worse.

—Teamsters Union boss Jimmy Hoffa, in 1957

During the second semester of my freshman year I made a mistake. I arranged for a fellow freshman friend of mine to take the examination for me. What I did was wrong. I have regretted it ever since.

—*Senator Edward Kennedy, on being caught for cheating at Harvard*

A liberal is a person with both feet firmly planted in the air.

—*writer Larry Wilde*

Being antiwar in Hollywood was an act of bravery on the order of the keynote speaker at a PLO dinner making jokes about Ariel Sharon.

—*Ann Coulter*

Maureen Dowd is an insecure, catty bitch.

—*blogger Markos Moulitsas,*
founder of Daily Kos

Many rich, politically active liberals spend their summers in France. Not for vacation, but for refresher courses in anti-Americanism.

—*Martin Higgins*

Protest noted. Now shut the hell up!

—bumper sticker

〜

Don't get the idea that I'm one of those goddamn radicals.

—gangster Al Capone

〜

The function of socialism is to raise suffering to a higher level.

—author Norman Mailer

〜

The NBA needs to start an affirmative-action program for short, slow white guys who can't jump.

—*writer J. J. Lane*

My generation of the sixties, with all our great ideals, destroyed liberalism, because of our excesses.

—*Camille Paglia*

A conservative is a person who comes to Bentonville, Arkansas, to study Wal-Mart and learn how to fix the post office. A liberal is a person who comes to Bentonville, Arkansas, to make Wal-Mart like the post office.

—Representative Newt Gingrich

I just wished Hurricane Katrina had only hit the United Nations building, nothing else, just had flooded them out, and I wouldn't have rescued them.

—Bill O'Reilly, host of The O'Reilly Factor

Liberal canon: reporting a falsehood often enough will make
it true.

—writer J. J. Lane

House Democratic Leader Nancy Pelosi proposed a New American
Plan Saturday. It raises the minimum wage, cuts student-loan rates,
and provides cheaper drugs. She's from San Francisco, where the four
basic food groups are Crosby, Stills, Nash, and Young.

—comic Argus Hamilton

She sweats a heck of a lot and looks well like an old eastern European hag without the makeup, made-up hair, and cute suits with pins.

> —*Wonkette.com, on former Secretary of State Madeleine Albright's gym habit*

It's "Bring Your Daughter to Work Day." This tradition began about twenty-five years ago down in Washington, D.C., by a quick-thinking Ted Kennedy who was spotted leaving his office with an eighteen-year-old.

> —*David Letterman*

Did you see Carter and Castro meeting together—dining together? The last time a president embraced a Cuban like that he got impeached.

—*Jay Leno*

Vegetarian—that's an old Indian word meaning "lousy hunter."

—*humorist Andy Rooney*

Senator Joe Lieberman's embrace with Bush immediately after the president's State of the Union address is known as the "Judas Kiss" among liberal Democrats who later went ape. Senator Hillary Clinton kissed Arafat's wife and they didn't make a peep. Which proves a very valuable lesson. Hot, girl-on-girl action is a non-starter for the Democratic Party.

—*Martin Higgins*

The liberals in the House strongly resemble liberals I have known
through the last two decades in the civil-rights conflict. When
it comes time to show on which side they will be counted, they
excuse themselves.

—*Representative Shirley Chisholm*

Hollywood liberals don't want to lose their source of income and still
be self-righteous. You know, have a dinner party at Barbra Streisand's
but spend an equal amount of time with the guests and out in the
kitchen talking to the Nicaraguans.

—*satirist Mort Sahl*

The Democratic constituency is just like a herd of cows. All you have to do is make a lot of noise, lay out the hay, and be ready to use the ole cattle prod in case a few want to bolt the herd.

—*James Carville*

On Wednesday, President Bush named the Justice Department headquarters after Robert F. Kennedy. Then he went around the corner and named a strip club after Ted.

—*Jay Leno*

Our major universities are now stuck with an army of pedestrian, toadying careerists, fifties types who wave around sixties banners to conceal their record of ruthless, beaver-like tunneling to the top.

—*Camille Paglia*

Eighty percent of the people who call themselves Democrats don't have a clue as to political reality.

—*James Carville*

As people do better, they start voting like Republicans—unless they have too much education and vote Democratic, which proves there can be too much of a good thing.

—*Karl Rove*

A lot of people say that this town is too liberal, out of touch with mainstream America, an atheistic pleasure dome, a modern-day, beachfront Sodom and Gomorrah, a moral black hole where innocence is obliterated in an endless orgy of sexual gratification and greed. I don't really have a joke here. I just thought you should know a lot of people are saying that.

—*Jon Stewart, hosting the Academy Awards*

A hippie is someone who looks like Tarzan, walks like Jane, and smells like Cheetah.

—President Ronald Reagan

Outside of the killings, Washington has one of the lowest crime rates in the country.

—former Washington, D.C., mayor Marion Barry

I've never been able to understand his appeal. Maybe his mother loved him, but I've never met anybody who does.

> —*Vice President Dick Cheney,*
> *on Democratic National Committee*
> *chairman Howard Dean, in an interview*
> *on Fox News'* Hannity & Colmes

I haven't committed a crime. What I did was fail to comply with the law.

> —*former New York City mayor David Dinkins,*
> *answering accusations that he failed to pay his taxes.*

I do know dumb-ass questions when I see dumb-ass questions.
—*Senator Orrin Hatch, speaking to Senator Chuck Schumer*

Republicans study the financial pages of the newspaper. Democrats put them in the bottom of the birdcage.
—*humorist Will Stanton, in*
Ladies' Home Journal (*1962*)

IV

THE ELECTION CYCLE

ELECTION CAMPAIGNS seem to have more in common with the rinse, wash, and spin cycles of laundromats than with voters reluctantly heading to the polls every two or four years. After Election Day, guess who is left out to dry. We are.

Candidates get their personal dirty laundry examined. As teams of consultants and media handlers use spot remover to remove the mud that's been slung, they are also busy crafting the spin.

How often do we hear "New and Improved!" from candidates seeking public office? At least it's now easy to separate the reds from the blues.

We're going to sell Jack like soap flakes.
—Joe Kennedy, on his son running for president in 1960

I actually did vote for the $87 billion before I voted against it.
—Democratic Party presidential nominee John Kerry, in 2004, explaining his stance on the Iraq War

When Kerry went duck hunting in early 2004, every hunter in America who wasn't already a Republican soon became one.
—Martin Higgins

I don't know why, but there's just something about Al Gore
that makes me laugh. My Al Gore was sort of like a gay
Gomer Pyle.

> —*mimic and comic Dana Carvey, on the* 2000
> *Democratic Party presidential nominee*

Q: How do you tell Al Gore from the Secret Service agents?
A: He's the stiff one!

> —*Anonymous*

When Bill Clinton blows his saxophone, America will be singing the blues.

                      —President George H. W. Bush,
                  during 1992 presidential campaign

Governor Clinton talks about change, change, change. Well that's all you're going to have in your pockets if he's elected.

                      —President George H. W. Bush,
                  during 1992 presidential campaign

Ozone Man, Ozone. He's crazy, way out, far out, man.
—President George H. W. Bush, on Democratic
Party Vice President nominee Al Gore during
the 1992 presidential campaign

All Norman Mailer, the politician, accomplished was to prove that in New York City almost anyone can get 41,000 votes if a million people go to the polls.
—columnist Richard Reeves, on the author's 1969 mayoral bid

Janet Reno lost the Democratic primary. When asked about it, Reno said, "I feel like I've been kicked in the nuts."

>   —*Conan O'Brien, on the former attorney general's*
>   *bid for governor of Florida.*

Janet Reno lost the primary election for governor down there in Florida. They think what hurt her were the allegations of steroid abuse.

>   —*David Letterman*

Have you ever tried to split sawdust?
> *—Senator Eugene McCarthy, asked if his running for*
> *president in 1968 would hurt the Democratic Party*

You know when I first thought I might have a chance? When I realized that you could go into any bar in the country and insult Lyndon Johnson and nobody would punch you in the nose.
> *—Senator Eugene McCarthy,*
> *on running for president in 1968*

They want me not only to bare my breast, but to go in for indecent exposure.

> —*Senator Eugene McCarthy, on ultra-left attacks during his 1968 presidential campaign*

Recession is when your neighbor loses his job. Depression is when you lose yours. And recovery is when Jimmy Carter loses his.

> —*Ronald Reagan, during the 1980 presidential campaign*

I'm just sick and tired of presidents who jog. Remember, if Bill Clinton wins, we're going to have another four years of his white thighs flapping in the wind.

—pundit Arianna Huffington, in 1996

To those critics who are so pessimistic about our country, I say: Don't be economic girly men.

—California governor Arnold Schwarzenegger, at the 2004 Republican National Convention

Bill Clinton and Al Gore represent the most pro-lesbian and pro-gay ticket in history.

—Pat Buchanan, in 1992

All the Chicago demonstrators wanted to do was to sleep in the park and kick policemen with razor blades in their shoes.

—Vice President Spiro Agnew, on riots at the 1968 Democratic National Convention

Kissing babies gives me asthma.

> —*John F. Kennedy, during his campaign for Congress in 1946*

I will slash my wrists and write an oath in blood that Jack will never run for vice president!

> —*Jacqueline Kennedy, speaking to friends at a dinner party in early 1960.*

Under the tousled boyish haircut it is still old Karl Marx.
—Ronald Reagan, in a letter to
Vice President Richard Nixon,
following John F. Kennedy's 1960
Democratic National Convention speech

My mother went into the Peace Corps when she was sixty-eight. My one sister is a motorcycle freak, my other sister is a Holy Roller evangelist, and my brother is running for president. I'm the only sane one in the family.

—Billy Carter, in 1976

Senator George McGovern was nominated by the cast of *Hair*.
> —*Representative Tip O'Neill, on the 1972 Democratic Party presidential nominee*

I am one thousand percent for Tom Eagleton and I have no intention of dropping him from the ticket.
> —*Senator George McGovern, shortly before dropping his vice presidential running mate*

It won't be a convention, but a coronation.
>   *—Frank Mankiewicz, McGovern aide, on the nomination*
>   *that sent the South Dakota senator toward the worst-ever*
>   *defeat in a U.S. presidential election*

For years, I wanted to run for president in the worst possible way—
and I'm sure I did.
>   *—Senator George McGovern, on his 1972 loss*

Lots of people are making fun of Katherine Harris, the Florida secretary of state. They're mainly making fun of her makeup, saying she doesn't know how to apply eye shadow or put on blush. This is just coming from Al Gore!

—*Jay Leno*

An Internet rumor claims that John Kerry had an affair with a young woman. When asked if this is similar to the Clinton/Lewinsky scandal, a spokesman said, "Close, but no cigar."

—*Jimmy Fallon*, Saturday Night Live's "Weekend Update"

If Barbara gets her hands on John Kerry, he might get another Purple Heart.

> —*former President George H. W. Bush,*
> *on his wife*

～

Once an election has been stolen in Cook County, it stays stolen.

> —*Mayor Richard Daley, in* 1960

～

This is the man who wants to be the commander-in-chief of our U.S. Armed Forces? Armed with what? Spitballs?

—Senator Zell Miller, on Democratic Party presidential nominee Senator John Kerry, in his 2004 Republican National Convention speech

Because the election was such a disaster for the Democrats, it looks like the leader of the party might be stepping down. But enough about Barbra Streisand.

—Jay Leno, in November 2004

You see the pictures in the paper today of John Kerry windsurfing? He's at his home in Nantucket this week, doing his favorite thing, windsurfing. Even his hobby depends on which way the wind blows.

—*Jay Leno, on the 2004 Democratic Party presidential nominee*

John Kerry says the "W" in George W. Bush stands for "Wrong." But he still can't explain what John Kerry stands for.

—*David Letterman, in 2004*

Kerry cares as much for national security as a giraffe.

—defense analyst Peter Huessy

John Kerry went duck hunting and he's doing that to fulfill his campaign pledge to hunt down the ducks and kill them wherever they are. Kerry did pretty well; he came back with four ducks and three Purple Hearts.

—David Letterman

I think nobody is truly qualified to be president of the
United States.

> —*Teresa Heinz Kerry, wife of 2004 Democratic
> presidential nominee, Senator John Kerry*

John Kerry announced a foolproof plan to wipe out the $500
billion deficit. John Kerry has a plan, he's going to put it on his
wife's Gold Card.

> —*Craig Kilborn, host of the
> Late Late Show, in 2004*

The Democratic machine in this country is putrid.

—*Teresa Heinz Kerry*

You said something I didn't say. Now shove it.

—*Teresa Heinz Kerry, to a* Pittsburgh Tribune-Review
reporter she claimed misquoted her

Kerry scored many points with voters and pundits by finally putting to rest criticism that he's a flip-flopper. Kerry said, "I have one position on Iraq: I'm *forgainst* it."

—*Amy Pohler,* Saturday Night Live's *"Weekend Update"*

During last night's debate, John Kerry and John Edwards were so friendly to each other some political experts think that they may end up running together. In fact, Kerry and Edwards were so friendly, President Bush accused them of planning a gay marriage.

—*Conan O'Brien, in 2004*

The president tends to have an attitude that unless you go all the way with LBJ, you don't go any of the way. He isn't going to get away with that with me.

—Richard Nixon, in 1966

People tell me that Senator Edwards got picked for his good looks, his sex appeal, and his great hair. I say to them, "How do you think I got the job?"

—Vice President Dick Cheney, on the 2004 Democratic Party vice presidential nominee

Not only are we going to New Hampshire. We're going to
South Carolina and Oklahoma and Arizona and North Dakota
and New Mexico, and we're going to California and Texas and
New York! And we're going to South Dakota and Oregon and
Washington and Michigan. And then we're going to Washington,
D.C., to take back the White House, Yeeeeeaaaaaargh!

*—Vermont Governor Howard Dean's high-decibel
remarks at the 2004 Iowa Caucuses after votes were counted*

I wanted to say to Governor Dean, don't be hard on yourself about
hooting and hollering. If I had spent the money you did and got 18
percent, I'd still be in Iowa hooting and hollering.

*—Reverend Al Sharpton,
on Howard Dean's Iowa scream*

So, how did Al Gore come to lose the presidential race? Simple. He ran. The ability to come across as warm and genuine to the American public is simply not in Al's *Westworld* wiring. "Al, you lost me at hello."

—Dennis Miller, in 2000

Walter Mondale has all the charisma of a speed bump.

—Will Durst, on the 1984 Democratic Party
presidential nominee

If elected, I will win.

—*comedian Pat Paulsen*

Two sporting events this past weekend were the Democratic debate and the Kentucky Derby. The winner was a long-shot gelding. As was also the case at the Derby.

—*Anonymous*

Wolf, be excited. This is "Joementum" here in New Hampshire.
—*Senator Joseph Lieberman, speaking to CNN anchor Wolf Blitzer, prior to the 2004 New Hampshire Democratic presidential primary*

This is the best election night in history.
—*Democratic National Committee chairman Terry McAuliffe, Nov. 2, 2004, just before 8 p.m. EST*

At every point in the campaign (save the first presidential debate) John Kerry was the candidate who had the embarrassing iconic moments: windsurfing, botox, fake tan, Swift Boats, Mary Cheney, $87 billion, saying f*ck in *Rolling Stone,* "global test," goose hunting. Every Dukakis-in-a-tank moment in this campaign belonged to Kerry.

—pundit Jonathan Last, on the 2004 election

One of my movies was called *True Lies.* It's what the Democrats should have called their convention.

—California Governor Arnold Schwarzenegger, in 2004

Run for office? No. I've slept with too many women, I've done too many drugs, and I've been to too many parties.

—*actor George Clooney*

This situation in Ohio would give an aspirin a headache.

—*Dan Rather, on the uncertainty*
of ballot results in 2004

I'm very familiar with the importance of dairy farming in Wisconsin. I've spent the night on a dairy farm here in Wisconsin. If I'm entrusted with the presidency, you'll have someone who is very familiar with what the Wisconsin dairy industry is all about.

—Democratic presidential nominee Al Gore, in 2000.

According to a new poll, Democrats are favoring Hillary Clinton for the Democratic presidential nominee for 2008. Democrats say they are looking for a fresh and exciting new way to get their asses handed to them.

—Tina Fey, Saturday Night Live's "Weekend Update"

Well, I lie all the time. I have to—to balance the family ticket.
—Lillian Carter, on her son Jimmy,
during the 1976 presidential race

I wouldn't bet the farm on it. I wouldn't even bet the outhouse on Mondale.
—Richard Nixon, on the Democratic Party
presidential nominee's chances against
Reagan in the 1984 presidential race

How they wanted Kerry to win! How they must be sunk in gloom in their caves and hideouts and seedy rented rooms! They knew that, for all his podium salutes and tough talk, Kerry would be another Jimmy Carter, another groveler, another guilt-addled, cringing apologizer for America's sins, past and present.

         —*columnist John Derbyshire, on the Democratic Party,*
                           following the 2004 election

V

POLITICAL
BONE PILE

HERE'S A USEFUL COLLECTION of all-purpose one-liners and observations that resist easy categorization. Some of these quotes are newly minted, while others date back to earlier periods in American history. You'll find that there's plenty of tasty meat left on these bones.

Everything is changing. People are taking their comedians seriously and the politicians as a joke.

—Will Rogers

If you want a friend in Washington, get a dog.

—President Harry S. Truman

I don't make jokes. I just watch the government and report
the facts.

—*Will Rogers*

America will never be destroyed from the outside. If we falter and
lose our freedoms, it will be because we destroyed ourselves.

—*President Abraham Lincoln*

Politics is the art of looking for trouble, finding it everywhere, diagnosing it incorrectly, and applying the wrong remedies.

—comedian Groucho Marx

The only difference between a taxman and a taxidermist is that the taxidermist leaves the skin.

—Mark Twain

Presidency, n. The greased pig in the field game of
American politics.

> —*Ambrose Bierce in* The Devil's Dictionary

I simply can't stand Washington. It's impossible to think or breathe in
the place.

> —*columnist Walter Lippman*

There are two things you need for success in politics. Money . . . and I can't think of the other.

—*Senator Mark Hanna*

Giving money and power to government is like giving whiskey and car keys to teenage boys.

—*P. J. O'Rourke*

There's a whole herd of sacred cows grazing in the lush green pastures of the federal government. Even though many of them quit giving milk long ago, we still fund them. I say take 'em out and shoot 'em.

—Senator Zell Miller

The most terrifying words in the English language are: I'm from the government and I'm here to help.

—President Ronald Reagan

Everyone is entitled to his own opinion, but not his own facts.

—*Senator Daniel Patrick Moynihan*

A politician is an animal which can sit on a fence and yet keep both ears to the ground.

—*H. L. Mencken*

Politics is the entertainment industry for ugly people.

—poet Mark Turpin

After two years in Washington, I often long for the realism and sincerity of Hollywood.

—Representative Fred Thompson, and actor

It is the first responsibility of every citizen to question authority.
—*Benjamin Franklin*

An honest politician is one who, when he is bought, will
stay bought.
—*Simon Cameron, Lincoln's first secretary of war*

One of the key problems today is that politics is such a disgrace;
good people don't go into government.

—real estate developer Donald Trump

Politics—all the excitement of chess and all the strategy of Bingo.

—Martin Higgins

A man who raises new issues has always been distasteful to politicians. He musses up what has been so tidily arranged.

—*Walter Lippman*

If you attack the establishment long enough and hard enough, they will make you a member of it.

—*Art Buchwald*

A politician's words reveal less about what he thinks about his subject than what he thinks about his audience.

—*columnist George F. Will*

A politician is one who talks himself red, white, and blue in the face.

—*Clare Boothe Luce*

The Senate is a nice, quiet sort of place where good representatives go when they die.

—Representative Thomas Reed

All I can say for the United States Senate is that it opens with a prayer and it ends with an investigation.

—Will Rogers

A palm-pounding pack of preening pols.
> —*former White House speechwriter and
> columnist William L. Safire, on Congress*

A politician will do anything to keep his job—even become
a patriot.
> —*publisher William Randolph Hearst*

Seen one president, you've seen them all.

—*Henry Kissinger*

When a man has cast his longing eye on offices, a rottenness begins in his conduct.

—*Thomas Jefferson*

Our public men are speaking every day on something—but they ain't saying anything.

—Will Rogers

The office of president is such a bastardized thing, half royalty and half democracy, that nobody knows whether to genuflect or spit.

—columnist Jimmy Breslin

The American presidency, it occurs to us, is merely a way station
en route to the blessed condition of being an ex-president.

—author John Updike

A straw vote only shows which way the hot air blows.

—author William Sydney Porter (O. Henry)

I think the most un-American thing you can say is, "You can't
say that."

—*writer and humorist Garrison Keillor*

Can any of you seriously say the Bill of Rights could get through
Congress today? It wouldn't even get out of committee.

—*attorney F. Lee Bailey*

I am a man of fixed and unbending principles, the first of which is to be flexible at all times.

—Senator Everett Dirksen

By 2000, politics will simply fade away. We will not see any political parties.

—futurist and thinker R. Buckminster Fuller, in 1966

The bottom line is, there have been a lot of nuts elected to the
United States Senate.

> —*Senator Charles Grassley*

If a politician murders his mother, the first response of the press will
likely be not that it was a terrible thing to do, but rather that in a
statement made six years before, he had gone on the record as being
opposed to matricide.

> —*columnist Meg Greenfield*

I believe there is something out there watching over us.
Unfortunately it's the government.

—filmmaker Woody Allen

If you see a snake, just kill it—don't appoint a committee
on snakes.

—Independent Party candidate and businessman Ross Perot

In our brief national history we have shot four of our presidents, worried five of them to death, impeached one, and hounded another out of office. And when all else fails, we hold an election and assassinate their character.

—*P. J. O'Rourke*

To announce that there must be no criticism of the president, or that we are to stand by the president right or wrong, is not only unpatriotic and servile, but is morally treasonable to the American public.

—*President Theodore Roosevelt*

What's the difference between a whore and a congressman?
A congressman makes more money.

—Edward Abbey

Politics is not a bad profession. If you succeed there are many
rewards. If you disgrace yourself you can always write a book.

—President Ronald Reagan

Politicians are like ships: noisiest when lost in a fog.
—humorist Bennett Cerf

In war, you can only be killed once, but in politics, many times.
—British Prime Minister Winston Churchill

Ninety percent of the politicians give the other 10 percent a
bad name.

—Henry Kissinger

Neither Beltway party is going to drain this swamp, because to
them it is not a swamp at all, but a projected wetland and their
natural habitat.

—Pat Buchanan

A Democrat sees the glass as half-empty. A Republican sees the glass as something that can be made cheaper in China.

—*comic John Higgins*

The American political system is like fast food—mushy, insipid, made out of disgusting parts of things, and everybody wants some.

—*P. J. O'Rourke*

Voting is simply a way of determining which side is the stronger without putting it to the test of fighting.

—*H. L. Mencken*

You can tell a lot about a fellow's character by the way he eats jelly beans.

—*President Ronald Reagan*

Politics, as a practice, whatever its professions, has always been the systematic organization of hatreds.

—historian Henry Adams

Suppose you were an idiot. Suppose you were a member of Congress. But I repeat myself.

—Mark Twain

When I see flags sprouting on official lapels, I think of the time in China when I saw Mao's *Little Red Book* on every official's desk, omnipresent and unread.

—Bill Moyers

Politicians are like diapers. They both need changing regularly and for the same reason.

—Anonymous

Under the Constitution of the United States, mimes have no First
Amendment rights.

—*Martin Higgins*

George Washington is the only president who didn't blame the
previous administration for his troubles.

—*Anonymous*

All great change in America begins at the dinner table.
—*President Ronald Reagan*

The twin disappointments of politics: knowing a candidate is incapable of performing the duties of the office and watching him dance at the inauguration.
—*Martin Higgins*

Hell, I never vote for anybody. I always vote against.

—comedian W. C. Fields

Life is one grand, sweet song, so start the music.

—President Ronald Reagan

VI

LAST
LAUGH

A man in a hot-air balloon realized he was lost. He reduced the altitude and spotted a woman below. He descended a bit more and shouted, "Excuse me, can you help me? I promised a friend I would meet him an hour ago, but I don't know where I am."

The woman below responded, "You must be a Democrat."

"I am," replied the balloonist, "but how did you know?"

"Well," said the woman, "you don't know where you are or where you are going. You have risen to where you are due to a large quantity of hot air. You made a promise that you have no idea how to keep, and you expect me to solve your problem. The fact is: you are in exactly the same position you were in before we met."

—Anonymous

ACKNOWLEDGMENTS

Without my good friend and editor, Bill K., who labored to pull this diverse material into coherence, I would still be sorting quotes and scribbling fulminations. Thanks to Father Larry Solan and my family at St. Mark Church for their prayers and kindness. Undying gratitude goes to Laura, my loving, long-suffering wife, for her encouragement and optimism, and also to my teen daughters, Brenna and Ayla, for cleaning the kitchen and doing a load of wash.

INDEX